Jack Prelutsky
Sweet &
Muppet Poems

Illustrated by Joe Ewers

A MUPPET PRESS/GOLDEN PRESS BOOK

Our Show

Our show should be terrific,
We practice all week long,
But when the curtain rises,
Almost everything goes wrong.

Sometimes the show is awful,
Sometimes it's even worse;
It hardly ever seems to go
The way that we rehearse.

The jokes are all forgotten
And the band sounds really weird;
Half the cast is missing
And the props have disappeared.

The dialogue is backward,
Someone tumbles on his face,
The stage is in a shambles,
It's an absolute disgrace.

Our bows are always clumsy,
It's a really sad display,
But since we do the best we can
It's probably okay!

Fozzie Bear?

Fozzie Bear?
Quite a guy
Porkpie hat
Big bow tie

Floppy ears
Bulbous nose
Clumsy feet
Crazy clothes

Goofy smile
Love to spare
Rotten jokes
FOZZIE BEAR!

Gonzo Will Do Anything

Gonzo will do anything,
He dreams up nutty stunts;
He's tried to catch a cannonball
And tried it more than once.

He's played the "Anvil Chorus"
While demolishing a car;
For Gonzo there is nothing
Too outrageous or bizarre.

He falls in love with chickens
And he wrestles with a brick.
He ate a rubber tire
And it didn't make him sick.

He tried to grow tomatoes
While he played the violin.
He danced on quarts of oatmeal—
What a mess when he fell in!

His unique imagination
Sets him very far apart.
Hanging spoons from his proboscis
Is his weird idea of art.

Though I think he has no talent
And I know he has no taste,
Gonzo also has no equal
And could never be replaced.

Miss Piggy

Miss Piggy doesn't like to be
Reminded of her age;
The one time Gonzo mentioned it,
She bounced him off the stage.

When Scooter accidentally said
He thought she was too fat,
She chased him for an hour
With a two-pound baseball bat.

When Fozzie told Miss Piggy
That her high notes were too shrill,
She raised a lump on Fozzie's head;
That lump is with him still.

If I decide to tell her
Things that aren't safe to say,
I'll tell her on the telephone
From fifty miles away.

My Garden

When the week is finally over,
It is wonderful to go
And putter in my garden
Where I watch the flowers grow.

It is pleasant in my garden
As I cultivate my seeds;
I plant and hoe and water
And I clear away the weeds.

Though it's frantic at the theater,
Here I leave that all behind,
And the calm within my garden
Gives this frog some peace of mind.